Remain Focused

To

The End

Abiola Awofadeju

Remain focused to the end.

Copyright © 2020 by Abiola Awofadeju

Under International Copyright Law, no part of this publication may be reproduced, stored in a retrieval system, or transmitted by any means electronic, mechanical, photographic or photocopy, recording or otherwise, without written permission from the publishers, except for brief quotation in critical reviews or articles.

All scriptures' quotations are taken from New King James version and as otherwise stated.

Published in United Kingdom by: Nikdam books.

E-mail: admin@nikdamconsulting.co.uk

Acknowledgement

I want to thank the Almighty God for the opportunity that He has given me to put this book together. It is by the grace of God, not that I am worthy, and I return all the glory back to Him.

My appreciation goes to my lovely husband for all the support I received throughout the period of putting this book together and his encouraging words.

Also, to my wonderful children for all their support, encouragement and checking on me time to time, during the writing and prompting me to complete this book.

My thanks go to Pastor F. Kasali and Mrs P. Ogri for taking time out of their busy schedules to proofread this book.

Lastly, I want to thank my siblings for believing in me and their support. All members of RCCG Power House Bristol, thank you. My prayer is that we will not look back, we will finish well and strong in Jesus Christ name, Amen.

Table of Content · Pages

Introduction	4 - 5
1. Be a child of God	6 - 9
2. Don't Look Back	10 - 13
3. Desire a better place	14 - 17
4. Lot's children	18 - 21
5. Storms of life	22 - 29
6. Steps to remain focus	30 - 33
Conclusion	34

INTRODUCTION

Beloved, I want to encourage you with the word of this book that you need to stand firm in the Lord. No matter what life may throw at you or whatever circumstances you may find yourself in at this moment, don't be distracted, remain focused. The plan of God for your life is great, greater than what you can imagine. His word in Jeremiah 29:11 says:

"for I know the thoughts that I think towards you, says the Lord, thoughts of peace and not of evil, to give you a future and a hope."

The same applies to your family and your expectation in God shall not be cut off. When you depend totally on God, He will give you the desires of your heart.

Do not give up on your dreams, persist and keep focusing on Jesus, who will bring it to pass. You need to persist until all goals are accomplished; do not give up on the way because faithful is He that has promised. He is not a man that He should lie or son of man that He should repent, whatever He promised He is able to bring it to pass.

So, keep waiting on the Lord and let your eyes remain focused on Him alone. Weeping may endure for a night, but joy comes in the morning. Remember, life is more than the lust of the flesh, the lust of the eye and the pride of life. All the things that we see are temporal, but the eternal things are full of value. Trial and temptation will come but God will not allow you to be tempted more than what you are able to bear, and He has said that He will make a way of escape.

In this world we are in now, it is easy to lose focus, to get distracted and caught up with things around us. This can cause us to forget our purpose in life and the reason for our creation, we are created to show forth God's glory and to worship God in the beauty of His holiness.

As we see in Hebrew 12:2a.

"looking away from all that will distract us and focusing our eyes on Jesus, who is the Author and Perfecter of faith."

Distraction will come but you must not allow it to stop you from running your race. Therefore, run the race that is set before you with your eyes focused on Christ alone, with perseverance to the end. Knowing fully that He who has called you is faithful.

To focus on Jesus simply means, concentrate on him alone and consciously remove your attention from things that can easily distract you. The more we focus on Jesus, the more our perspective about worldly things changes. This enables us to think more about Jesus. How to please Him and be like Him will take priority in our lives more than anything else.

CHAPTER ONE

BE A CHILD OF GOD

God has a plan for His children and in order to receive all that God has for you, you need to be one of his children. You need to receive Jesus Christ as your Lord and personal saviour. You need to acknowledge your sins, confess and forsake them, promise God not to go back to that old way of life and decide to follow Jesus Christ to the end. Romans 3:23 says:

"For all have sinned and fallen short of the glory of God,"

and 1 John 1:8-9 also says,

"if we say we have no sin, we deceive ourselves, and the truth is not in us. If we confess our sins, He is faithful and just to forgive us our sins and cleanse us from all unrighteousness."

Agreed that you are one of His, and that you have confessed Jesus Christ as your Lord and Saviour, You, however, need to remain focused on Him. Your eyes need to be fixed on Him; not moving to and through aimlessly, like one that has no direction. The sins of the past must not trap you down, repent of those sins sincerely and ask the blood of Jesus to cleanse you. Be determined not to sin anymore but press on looking unto Jesus Christ, your Saviour.

Looking at the story of Lot and his family in the Word of God, God had a great plan for Lot and his family; but due to the attitude of Lot's wife, she jeopardised the plan of God for her and her family. This is why the Word of God says in Proverb 14:1 that,

"The wise woman builds her house, but the foolish pulls it down with her hands."

A woman can only be wise when she remains focused on God and also the same applies to the man. Lot's wife got distracted so easily with the things of the world, she would not let go. She allowed the pleasures of the world and the things that were in it, to take the place of God.

Lot was Abraham's nephew, brought up by Abraham, but when God was about to destroy Sodom and Gomorrah, He informed Abraham. Genesis 18:22-23 says,

"Then the men turned away from there and went toward Sodom, but Abraham still stood before the Lord. And Abraham came near and said, "Would You also destroy the righteous with the wicked?"

Abraham started negotiating with God, stood in the gap and interceded on behalf of Lot and his family. This was why Lot and his family were rescued from the destruction that fell upon Sodom and Gomorrah. Lot was brought up by Abraham as said earlier, he was taught in God's way and this showed in Abraham's conversation with God, asking God to spare the righteous from the wicked. Knowing fully that Lot and his family will be counted among the righteous and escape the judgement that came upon Sodom. God heard Abraham's prayer and saved Lot and his family.

Abraham was a man that relied totally on God; he trusted God and never waved at God's promises. He remained focused in all situations and was counted faithful. God has never changed,

"Jesus Christ is the same yesterday, today and forever," Hebrew 13:8.

If only we can call upon God in all situations, put our trust totally on Him and remain focused till the end, not casting away our confidence in Him which has a great reward, He will surely fulfil His promises in our lives.

The question is, when trials of faith and temptations come, would you remain focused on God as Abraham did? Trials come from God and they are designed to prove our faith in Christ, but temptation comes from the devil and our uncrucified flesh to lure us to sin against God. Our attitude during trials and temptations will reveal our stand in the Lord, whether these will shift our focus from following the Lord or not.

Consistently losing victory over trials and temptations can cause one to lose focus on following Jesus to the end. As ones' faith in Christ can be shaken by given chance to doubt and doubting the ability of Jesus Christ to save and deliver, this can ruin the original plan and purpose of God for an individual. The Devil can use this opportunity of doubting to strike and cause the individual to lose focus on Jesus and thereby resolve to an alternative solution. Therefore, the Word of God encourages believers in the following Scriptures not to allow doubt in dealing with God, James 1:6 says,

"But let Him ask in faith, with no doubting, for he who doubts is like a wave of the sea driven and tossed by the wind,"

Also, Romans 14:23 says,

" but he who doubts is condemned if he eats, because he does not eat from faith; for whatever is not from faith is sin."

So, whatever that is not from faith is sin but uncompromising faith in the Lord Jesus Christ serves as an ingredient that will help us to remain focused to the end.

CHAPTER TWO

Don't Look Back

Lot's wife looked back and became a pillar of salt.

How? Genesis 19:15-17 and 26,

"When the morning dawned, the angels urged Lot to hurry, saying, "arise, take your wife and your two daughters who are here, lest you be consumed in the punishment of the city. "And while he lingered, the men took hold of his hand, his wife's hand, and the hands of his two daughters, the Lord being merciful to him, and they brought him out and set him outside the city. So, it came to pass, when they had brought them outside, that he said, "Escape for your life! Do not look behind you nor stay anywhere in the plain. Escape to the mountains, lest you be destroyed." But His wife looked back behind him, and she became a pillar of salt."

There is an instruction here, Lot and his family were told to escape for their lives and that they should not look back. Why? There are lots of spiritual implications for looking back when God is telling you to go forward. To look back means to shift away your attention, your focus from God's plan and purpose but gaze into the world of vanity. Instead of looking back, Jesus admonishes believers to look unto Him the author and finisher of our faith. Also, the Psalmist says that,

"His own looked unto Him and were radiant, and their faces were not ashamed," Psalm 34:5.

The more you look unto Jesus, the more you will be changed from glory to glory and your face will remain radiant till the end. Also, when you look unto Jesus, He is the only one that can give you perfect liberty. See what the Scripture says in James 1:25,

"But he who looks into the perfect law of liberty and continues in it and is not a forgetful hearer but a doer of the work, this one will be blessed in what he does."

So, Jesus Christ is that perfect law of liberty that a believer should continually look unto to remain free from the devil and his cohorts.

In essence, Lot's wife looked back because she was not conversant with perfect law of liberty (Jesus Christ), that brings hope when all hope is lost but focused more on the things that were temporal, things that were unable to deliver her when trials and temptations came.

In Psalm 119:37, David prayed to God and said,

"turn my eyes from looking at worthless things and give me life in your way."

David knew somethings that can distract one from gazing on Jesus Christ and these things are worthless. This is the reason he prayed like this and because he knew His God as the author and finisher of his faith. Whoever knows this God, like David, will be strong and do exploits. Immediately Lot's wife looked behind, she became a pillar of salt and her destiny was truncated. This was disobedient to God's instruction which carries great consequences.

Perhaps, you may want to ask yourself this question: why did Lot's wife look back? What was she looking for at that moment? The answer is this, Lot's wife found it difficult to let go of Sodom and Gomorrah, what she had acquired there, money, wealth, houses, friends, worldly pleasures and so forth. She had forgotten that the bible admonishes believers not to remember the former things, encourages us to forget what is past and put that behind.

Many times, the past serves as an obstacle to a greater tomorrow. Nobody makes it great by dwelling in the past and slaves of the past are always miserable in life. Past achievements and successes should not become a snare to our greater tomorrow.

Likewise, past defects, failures and disappointments should not make you bitter, angry and shift your attention from God. Get rid of the negative past and move on to the glorious future that Jesus has for you. Apostle Paul says,

"This one thing I do forgetting those things which are behind and reaching forth unto those things which are before". I press toward the mark for the prize of the high callings of God in Christ Jesus," Philippians 3:13-14.

As a believer of today, continuous pressing forward in the things of God will help you to stay focused on Jesus Christ to the end of your journey in life. God is telling you today, to forget where you are coming from, forget your past achievements, those things that were behind, that can draw you back to the world and those things that can hinder you from moving forward or doing the will of God, listen to God's voice today and you will have good success.

Example of a believer that remained focused on God despite what life threw at her, was the slave girl in Naaman's house. She was battered with the yoke of slavery but in the midst of this, she was able to recommend the God of Israel to her master. She knew the God of Israel is a deliverer, a healer if only her master Naaman could seek help from Him, that He would deliver him of his leprosy. 2King 5:1-14.

The slave girl became a source of blessing to her boss, to her master's household and changed her master's story from being a leper to a brand-new person. This is what God has called us to, to remain focus in all situations of life. Difficult and challenging time, when it is good or bad, challenging times will come but you should not allow these to shift your focus from following the Lord, hold on to what you believe about God who has called you and promises you hope of glorious ending.

The word of God in 2 Cor 4:17 says,

"For our light affliction, which is but for a moment, is working for us a far more exceeding and eternal weight of glory."

Brethren, stay focus know that your present trials are for a moment, as you allow God to have His way, things will work out good in your favour too.

CHAPTER THREE

DESIRE A BETTER PLACE

Moreover, God does not want you to lose focus on Him because He has a place for you, a better place that Jesus Christ has for His own people, who will endure to the end. Saying this, He is telling you to desire a better place because the world has nothing good to offer. Abraham desired a better place in God, He obeyed when he was asked to leave his country, his people, to an unknown destination. He doubted not, He did not wave at God's promises. He counted God faithful who had promised, for he was fully persuaded and looked forward to that city that has foundations, whose designer and builder is God (Hebrew 11:10).

"Having these promises "let us hold fast the confession of our hope without wavering, for He who promised is faithful," Hebrew 10:23.

The promise of a new city, a new Jerusalem, which awaits the uncompromised saint in the Lord Jesus, those who have left everything that the world can offer and have determined to hold on to Jesus Christ to the end.

The Scripture also bears witness to this city in Hebrew 11:15-16 that:

"if they had longed for the country they came from, they could have gone back. But they were looking for a better place, a heavenly homeland."

They were looking forward to a new Jerusalem, the fathers of faith made a conscious effort to forget where they came from and quickly embraced a better country and the heavenly one. Therefore, God is not ashamed to be called their God: for they have endured all things because of the name of Jesus.

Isn't this wonderful? God prepared for them a city and not an ordinary place. God has a better place for His own people, a future and a glorious end. On the point that you do not lose focus, not compromise your faith in God and not create another altar beside Him. His promise remains valid to give you the desired end. Remember that whoever lays his hand on the plough and looks back, such a person is not fit for the kingdom. I pray that you will not look back, you will stand firm in the faith to the end, and you will not fall or fail God in Jesus' name.

Abraham came from an idolatry family but chose to follow God. Moses was not happy to enjoy the pleasure of sins, but rather chose to suffer affliction with the people of God. Rahab was a harlot but having seen the wonders of the God of Israel, she chose to hide the people of God that came to spy the land of Jericho in order to save her life and that of her family. Peter left his fishing career to follow Jesus and became a fisher of men and Paul left everything to follow Christ. To mention but a few, these were mighty men of God, who God poured His abundant grace upon and used them as a vessel of honour, mighty instruments of blessings; having forgotten who they were, they followed Jesus Christ to the end.

It is my earnest prayer that you will let go of who you are and come to take refuge under the arms of the Almighty God. Be like David in Psalm 46:1 that says,

"God is my refuge and strength, a very present help in trouble."

Jesus Christ is the only available help that anyone can have at any given time. When situations of life are good or bad, when you are at the edge of giving up in life, He is always there to run to. He never slumbers nor sleep; He is an Advocator, a Deliverer, a Healer, a helper, Sustainer, Way Maker, our banner, our shield and so on.

Therefore, run the race that is set before you with patience, leaning on God's grace and mercy to the end. This is the reason Paul said in 1Timothy 6:7 that:

"for we have brought nothing into the world, so [it is clear that] we cannot take anything out of it either."

Fully aware of this, He set his mind on Jesus Christ to the end, not on material things or what the world can offer. He learnt to concentrate on Jesus, focusing on His word and fully engaged in His service.

In Proverb 30:7-9, there is a prayer that says:

"Two things have I required of thee; deny me not before I die: remove far from me vanity and lies; give me neither poverty nor riches; feed me with food convenient for me: lest I be full and deny thee, and say, who is the Lord? Or lest I be poor, and steal, and take the name of God in vain."

My prayer is that you will not deny the Lord, you will not be full and forget who the Lord is. You will always be satisfied with the abundance that the Lord will provide for you from His table.

Here, the proverb is simply saying that God should give him just enough to satisfy His needs. When you are dining at the Lord's table every time, He will satisfy your needs and your longing soul will be refreshed daily in His presence. As long as you do not get distracted from His presence and you meditate daily on His word, the Almighty God promises in Psalms 1:3 that.

"You will be like a tree planted by the rivers of water. That brings forth its fruit in its season, whose leaf also shall not wither; And whatsoever he does shall prosper."

CHAPTER FOUR

What Happened to Lot's Children?

Does God's plan remain valid after Lot's wife got distracted? Yes, His word has found yes in Him.

In Numbers 23:19, the word of God says,

"God is not a man, so He does not lie, He is not human, so he does not change his mind. Has he ever spoken and failed to act? Has he ever promised and not carried it through?"

This means that whatever God says or promises, He will bring it to pass. Unfortunately, Lot's daughter got distracted along the way and took an important decision of a lifetime with a levity hand. They lacked good and godly counsel, they had shifted their focus away from God of plan and purpose.

So, God's plan was hindered by the actions of Lot's daughters, having depended on their knowledge and they based their decision on what was happening around them instead of seeking godly counsel. The mother was not there anymore to train and teach them in the way of the Lord. And this is especially important as the bible encourages us:

"to train up a child in the way he should go, even when he is old, he will not depart from it," Proverb 22:6

Lot's wife was no more, to guide her children in the way of the lord, when the children needed her most. She disobeyed God by not listen to the instruction given by the Angels. The bible warns believers about the love of the world, that it is an enmity with God. You cannot serve God and Belial.

Lot's wife lose focus, she could not let go of Sodom and Gomorrah. She did not make progress; she looked back and became a pillar of salt. Lot's daughters were unable to live a life of testimony and unable to fulfil destiny. Their action to sleep with their father was a great abomination in the history of the bible. Let's imagine the kind of thought that occupied their mind; when they were supposed to set their minds on the things above and engaged in the service of God, they were busy looking for how to get their father drunk, so that they can preserve their family line.

Who does that, thinking sleeping with their dad was the only way their family line could be preserved? God works in a mighty way and He knows how to make a way out in the wilderness of life. If only they had focused on God for solution, they wouldn't have preserved seed through sin. This was not a surprise because their foundations were already destroyed and if the foundation be destroyed, what can the righteous do? And the same God says in Hebrew 13:4 that,

" marriage is honourable among all, and the bed undefiled, but fornicators and adulterers God will judge."

Impatience, losing focus and inability to know God's mind, His plan and purpose for one's life can lead to problems that can destroy the future.

As a child of God, our lives are supposed to reflect the glory of God. Let us teach our children in the way of the Lord, to love and fear the Lord. Be a light in the midst of their dark world, lead them to Jesus. Put your best in to see that they have a personal relationship with the Lord and when they do so, great shall be their peace. Such a child will not depart from the truth. Any child who receives Jesus as his or her Lord and personal saviour early in life, will know where to seek help when trials and temptations of life comes and he or she will not give up on God.

Psalm 37:4-5 says:

"Delight yourself also in the Lord, and He shall give you the desires of your heart. Commit your ways to the Lord, trust also in Him, and He shall bring it to pass."

When God says delight yourself in Him, He is simply saying concentrate on Him, keep focusing on Him in all circumstances and as you do so, your desires will be in line with God's perfect will for your life and He will surely bring them to pass.

Losing trust in God's ability for breakthrough in life will lead to failure. Such a person, like Lot's daughters, can adopt any ungodly supplement or way out for his or her unpleasant situation, leaving Jesus Christ out of the way. Brethren, do not lose confidence in God due to impatience, let patience have its due course in your life.

Nothing in this world should make us lose focus on Jesus Christ - the solid foundation. God wants you to trust Him completely, never seek solution or help from the devil and his agents because the bible says in Psalm 16:4 that:

"Troubles multiply for those who chase after other gods. I will not take part in their sacrifices of blood or even speaks the names of their gods."

It is my prayer that you will always seek after God and you will not be partaker of any troubles meant for those that say that they do not do God.

CHAPTER FIVE

Storms of Life.

Looking back will not solve the problem or stop the storm you are passing through. Apostle Paul made up his mind after his encounter with God, never to go back to the world. He counted all things but loss for the excellency of the knowledge of Christ. He was ready to suffer for Jesus Christ's sake. He remained focused despite all he passed through.

There are lots of things that can cause one to lose focus, as revealed in the life of Lot and his family. People of God are still prone to the same trials and temptation today. If in all these, we are able to hold on to our profession of faith without wavering, we are more than a conqueror through Christ who strengthens us.

Other things that can cause you to lose focus are the followings:

FEAR OF THE UNKNOWN
Lot exercised fear of the unknown in his journey of life and this contributed to the failure of his daughters. How? In Genesis 19:17,

"So, it came to pass when they had brought them outside, that he said, "Escape for your life! Do not look behind you nor stay anywhere in the plain. Escape to the mountains, lest you be destroyed."

This was the original plan of God for Lot and his family. In verse 18-22, then Lot said to them,

"Please, no, my Lords! Indeed now, your servant has found favour in your sight, and you have increased your mercy which you have shown me by saving my life; but I cannot escape to the mountains, lest some evil overtake, and I die. See now, this city is near enough to flee to, and it is a little one; please let me escape there (is it not a little one?) and my soul shall live."

We can see from this conversation between the Lord and Lot that the original plan of God for Lot's family was to escape to the mountain, but due to the fear of the unknown, Lot appealed to go elsewhere. Lot was so engrossed with the fear of the unknown and this made him settle down for the less, which later affected the lives of his daughters. Setting alternatives for God is not an option. Do not look for quick and easy ways especially when God has designed a way out of your situation.

Another thing is that fear brings torment, and this is one of the reasons why the words of God always encourage believers to fear not. In whatever situation that you may find yourself, God is saying fear not and He will help you. God has not given you the spirit of fear, but of sound mind, whereby you cry unto Him, Abba father.

LOST OF HOPE

Hopelessness may affect your decision to keep your eyes focused on God. If you are believing God for a breakthrough in one area of your life and it seems there is a delay in achieving the desired result, you may find yourself losing faith in God. Do not lose faith. God assures believers, especially you, of His ever-present help in times of need. The statement, "I am with thee" serves as comforting words to the helpless and hopeless situations the Israelites found themselves in when they were in Babylon.

Although there is this gross darkness that surrounds those that are in helpless and hopeless situations, there is also this comfort in the midst of darkness; the Almighty, the all-knowing, and the ever-present help that God gives to His own children, whose minds stay on Him. He said, "He will keep in perfect peace whose mind stayed on Him". Those that will not allow the situations of life to cause them to lose focus on following Jesus Christ to the end. In the book of Psalm 46:1-2,5, the bible says,

Jesus Christ is "------ A very present help in trouble", Therefore we will not fear, even though the earth be removed, and though the mountains be carried into the midst of the sea; (5) God is in the midst of her, she shall not be moved. God shall help her, just at the break of dawn."

My prayer is that hope will spring forth in your situation because the Almighty will help you. Amen. In Job 14:7 the bible also says, *"for there is the hope of a tree, if it is cut down, that it will sprout again, and that the tender branch thereof will not cease."*

No matter how hopeless your situation appears to be, if you put your hope in Jesus and remain focused on Him, He will surely turn that situation around for good in a way that is beyond your imagination and human understanding.

LACK OF VISION OF WHERE YOU ARE GOING.

People perish because of lack of knowledge. A man lacks knowledge or a vision in life when there is nothing to drive him towards achieving any goal. He will continue to wonder, standstill or even turn back. A believer with no vision of heavenly home will perish in the midst of adversity, failure and discouragement of life. Elijah tried to discourage Elisha from following him when he was about to leave the earth, but, because Elisha had set a focus on receiving a double portion of Elijah's power, he refused to be stopped.

Also, the sons of the prophets teased and mocked him that his master will be taken away from him. Despite all these, Elisha refused to be discouraged nor lose focus; he went ahead to achieve the desired result, because he persisted and determined to the end.

When you have a vision of enjoying the kingdom of God here on earth and in heaven, you will not allow anybody or circumstances of life to shift your attention from following

Jesus. This is because you know that He that promised, is faithful and He will bring it to pass. Habakkuk 2: 2-3,

"Then the Lord answered me and said: write the vision and make it plain on the tablets, that he may run who reads it. For the vision is yet for an appointed time, but at the end, it will speak, and it will not lie. Though it tarries, wait for it; because it will surely come, it will not tarry."

The visions came to pass in the life of faithful believers of old. People like Sarah, Hannah, Simeon, Elizabeth, and Ruth the Moabites achieved their set goals. The Lord visited them at the appointed time, at the time of life. This same God is still the same today, working all things in your favour, because He says all things will work together for your good for those that love Him and walk according to His will. Therefore, as you set your mind on Him and do not lose hope, His plan will come to fulfilment in your life.

LACK OF STRENGTH TO CARRY ON
To remain focused on God, you must be strong in Him. There is no room for weakness or laziness because the bible let us know in Ephesians 6:12,

"for we do not wrestle against flesh and blood, but against powers, against the rulers of the darkness of this age, against spiritual hosts of wickedness in the heavenly places."

The enemy is waging war against believer's day and night. He is looking for loopholes, where he can attack, since his mission is to steal, to kill and to destroy. This is the why the bible encourages believers to remain strong. God is a God of encouragement and consolation. He is the father of mercy and the God of all comforts. He knows that the enemy will want to hinder believers with fear.

Joshua was fearful when He took over the leadership of Israel, but the Almighty God encouraged him to be strong and be courageous. Joshua took courage from the word of God and did exploits for God. Believers are to be strong in the Lord and remain focused on Him to the end. No matter the task, remember that you can do all things through Christ that strengthens you. No matter the spiritual battles you are facing,

"You are more than conquerors through Christ that loves you," Romans 8:37.

always wait on the Lord for a renewal of strength. Do not depend on your own ability because your strength may fail, but God never fails. The battle we face as Christians is purely spiritual warfare. This warfare requires courage to withstand dreadful circumstances, determination to overcome at all costs, persistent prayer and fully focus on Jesus in order for us to overcome.

Apostle Paul said He has fought and won the race. This will be your testimony at the end in Jesus' name. You will not fall or fail in the battles of life; you will be an overcomer in Jesus' name.

PRESENT CHALLENGES OF LIFE.

The present challenges of life may want to cause one to lose focus. One thing to do is to realise that there is more to what you are passing through now. Hear what the Scripture says in 2 Corinthians 4:7,

"Knowing fully that the present affliction, which is but for a moment, is working for you a far more exceeding and eternal weight of glory."

Hallelujah! Affliction, problems, challenges of life will not last forever, they are for a moment. They are transient and temporary and surely, there will be an end to them if you do not give up on God: knowing fully that everyone who has been born of God overcomes the world and this is the victory that overcomes the world, even our faith.

It takes the grace of God to remain focused when facing different challenges in life. The prevalence of evil things happening around the world today are other challenges people are facing, but those who have determined to follow Jesus Christ to the end, will surely overcome them if they do not turn back.

Brethren, what happened in Sodom and Gomorrah is happening in our world today. Apostle Paul told us of some things that can shake a believer's faith. One of these is the challenges of life, which can manifest themselves in the form of the financial crisis and health issues. People are dying daily because of poverty and different kinds of diseases and viruses. Others include homelessness, the killing of people because of their faith in Jesus Christ, terrorisms here and there and many others. All these can cause people to lose their focus on Jesus Christ, but we have to refuse to be distracted.

We should not be discouraged by everything that is happening because this will happen towards the end. And at a time like this, according to the word of God, people will be lovers of evil rather than a lover of God and righteousness. Apostle Paul asked this question in Romans 8:35 that:

"who shall separate us from the love of Christ? shall tribulation or anguish, or persecution, or famine, or nakedness, or peril or sword?"

And in Romans 8:38-39, he answered it by saying:

"for I am persuaded that neither death nor life, nor angels nor principalities nor powers, nor things present nor things to come, nor height nor depth, nor any other created thing, shall be able to separate us from the love of God which is in Christ Jesus our Lord."

You should not allow any of these things to separate you from the love of God that is in Christ Jesus. Let it be your prayer and determination that you will focus on Jesus and that no situations of life will separate you from His love.

CHAPTER SIX

King David remained focused.

King David in the bible is an example of someone who remained focused on God to the end and enjoyed the reward of faithfulness. King David learnt how to depend on God in all circumstances of life; whether things were good or bad, he always went to God to inquire on what to do. So, he relied solely on God's direction. 1Samuel 30:1-8.

Also, King David knew how to draw strength from God through His word. He knew how to ascribe all the glory back to God, he never shared in God's glory. An addicted worshipper of God, he cherished being in the presence of God more than being in the presence of the mere human. No wonder that it was recorded on account of King David, that he was a man after God's heart.

People of God, from today on, be determined to remain a conqueror, stand firm, remain focused, be bold and have strong faith in God. No matter what life throws at you, stay victorious and a winner. God of all comfort will comfort you and give you your desired request in Jesus Christ name (AMEN), 1Corithians 15:58,

"therefore, my beloved brethren, be steadfast, immovable, always abounding in the work of the lord, knowing that your labour is not in vain in the lord."

What to do to Remain focus on Jesus Christ.

You can remain focused through reading, studying and meditating on God's word. John 5:39 says,

"to search and keep on searching and examining the Scriptures because you think that in them you have eternal life, and yet it is those [very Scriptures] that testify about Jesus."

It is the word of God that testifies about Jesus, and as you meditate on the word, you are being changed and transformed to the image of Jesus Christ. Keep on searching and examining the word of God.

Joshua 1:8 says:

"This book of the law shall not depart from your mouth, but you shall meditate in it day and night, that you may observe to do according to all that is written in it. For then you will make your way prosperous, and then you will have good success."

Engaging more in the word of God, makes you reason and think like Jesus, and you will not be able to gratify the desires of the flesh. Your mind will be set on high, on things that will please Him and your attention will always be in His presence. And as you think of God's word, which is Jesus, you become like Him and it will be difficult for you to lose track of focusing on Him.

You can remain focused on Him by putting your faith into action. How? When you have faith in God and his ability to do all things, you will fix your eyes on Him to the end. You will believe His words that they are yes and amen, you will not doubt His words even, in difficult times. When men forsake you, you will not be moved because you will know that you have a high Priest which is touched by whatever that you may be passing through. He says in Hebrew 4:15,

"for we have not a high priest which cannot be touched with the feeling of our infirmities but was in all points tempted like we are, yet without sin."

Another way that can help you to remain focused on Jesus is to be content in Christ, because godly contentment has a great reward.

As seen in 1 Timothy 6:6, *"But godliness with contentment is a great gain."*

The only place you can find true fulfilment and contentment is in acceptance of Jesus Christ as your Lord and personal Saviour. Allowing your conviction of knowing Jesus to govern your sense, that Christ's power, purpose and provision is sufficient in all your circumstances. This will enable you to learn to walk through all kinds of adversity, believing and experiencing Christ's sufficiency, focusing on Him to the end.

In addition, Prayer without ceasing helps to focus more on Jesus. Prayer is a two-way communication; you commune with God and God does the same. When you commune with God, you are fellowshipping with Him and through this act, you are concentrating on Jesus; fixing your eyes on Him, telling Him that you depend totally on Him alone because His word says in Philippians 4:6

"Do not be anxious about anything, but in every situation, by prayer and petition, with thanksgiving present your request to God."

Make all your requests known unto God in the place of prayer and God that you prayed to in secret will answer you openly. Add to your prayer a consistent life of fasting: for without prayer and fasting some important blessings you desired, may be difficult to achieve.

CONCLUSION

Therefore, brethren let your eyes remain on Him alone and focus on Jesus Christ to the end. Refuse to be like Lot's wife, who lost focus because of the pleasure of the world. She was not able to make progress; she lost it and lost everything.

Please, dear reader presses on to the mark of the high calling that is in Christ Jesus and He will sustain and see you through. See that you do not get distracted from Him (Jesus Christ). You have received a kingdom that cannot be shaken, let us ask for grace by which we may serve God acceptably with reverence and godly fear.

www.ingramcontent.com/pod-product-compliance
Lightning Source LLC
Chambersburg PA
CBHW071550080526
44588CB00011B/1857